SEDGEMOOR

To Jackie, Daniel and Louise

Thanks are due to the editors of *Envoi, South* and *The Interpreter's House,* where some of these poems were first published.

SEDGEMOOR

Malcolm Povey

Published 2006
by

Smokestack Books
PO Box 408, Middlesbrough TS5 6WA
e-mail : info@smokestack-books.co.uk
www.smokestack-books.co.uk

Cover design by James Cianciaruso

Printed by
EPW Print & Design Ltd

ISBN 0955106133

Smokestack Books
gratefully acknowledges the support of
Middlesbrough Borough Council
and Arts Council North East

Smokestack Books is a member of
Independent Northern Publishers
www.northernpublishers.co.uk
and is represented by Inpress Ltd
www.inpressbooks.co.uk

Contents

Cheers

To Monmouth! His health!'
A pub stoolie reported
The Scots Guard pledging,
Knocking back ale with his mates
Prior to riding to the West Country
To fight said Duke and rebs.
Though given tavern clatter, song,
The Scots accent in Cockney ears
Yet to be coached by Rab C. Nesbit,
And given the possibility of irony,
Monmouth's 'health' being a sword in his ribs,
His 'health' the five grand reward
For wielder of sword, it's a dodgy story.

Not that the court considered irony.
Three regiments paraded to observe
'This is what we do to scrots like you'.
They hanged two Guards till dead,
'The other was whipped, standing with a rope
About his neck beneath the gallows'.
All played their parts in the theatre of war.

And in 1948, my soldier-dad's driver,
In disputed Trieste, knocking back his espresso,
Pledged 'Viva Italia' walking out the door,
With a provocative, digital gesture.

They found him, hours later,
Shot through the head down an alley,
His tonality gone with his breath.

Careless words, and I guess,
If you lifted your brandy glass
'To Clinton! His health!'

In a Belgrade bar, as the bombs
Pick their way in satin slippers
Across the darkened stage of night,
You might get more than you bargain for.

By Cart to Battle

The cart, big and strong as a pick-up truck,
Wood wheels banging, is crammed
With stale bread, sequestered scythes
To beat and sharpen flat. Cider, to blur
And provoke, drips through gaps.

The driver, big and strong as a pick-up truck,
Set forth conquering and to conquer,
Sees the scarlet whore of Babylon in Moll,
Hedge-back trollop, would whip
And use her lustily.

The lad, cracking his hazel switch
Above heaving haunches, sings praise
Of Monmouth, his good cheer and flag
Of Christ, high on not stone-picking,
Not herding sheep.

The girl, watching their noisy struggle,
Admires the lad's blonde sheen,
Taps a bare foot to his tune,
Wondering who will get the harvest in,
Now scythe and scyther are gone.

Mother

I feed the hens, then fat our pig.
I sweep the yard and pray and pray
The Lord my oldest son to keep
Safe. Keep whole. My favourite
Is gone to fight, my father's sword,
Which struck so hard in Cromwell's cause,
Swings at his side. My woven cloth
Will warm his back. My chuck. He laughs
Astride, at six, our mastiff's back.
He cries, aflush with fever, an owl
Claws him wood-ward, a hanging mouse.
I prayed: the Lord restored his life.

They say he marches godly strong.
They say the Son of God protects,
Will slap away blood-seeking balls
Like midges. I dream each night
A grassy field bleeds sogging red.
I dream the owl returned to hunt
My son. I wish he had not gone.
I wish him singing at the loom.

First Sign: Lyme Regis, 13 June 1685

Dare, hothead merchant,
Rides a fine stallion
Foraged from Prideaux,
Heads a troop of horse
He's raised to fight Papists,
Thunders forty strong
Into a Lyme of cheers,
Prayer and drilling men.

Fletcher of Saltoun,
Monmouth's best officer,
Colonel of Horse,
Eyes the fine charger,
Trade on its back,
Claims it his battle-ride.

'Fuck off and find yer own:
Not your nose in the air
Like some fucking gentry
Toss-pot I'm fighting for.'

Or words to that effect,
Words as now lost
As weavers' words wrought,
When, straightening scythe
For pike, learning to load
And fire the latest flintlocks,
Seeking a sign that The Lord

Backs them, and will guide
Unmartial hands in battle,
They look up to see Fletcher,
Glory-sashed, pull his pistol out
And kill stick-thwacking Dare.

First casualty:
First sign.

Dare's son demands revenge.
Somerset weavers demand
Fletcher hang for killing
Their man from Taunton.

Monmouth, army-man,
Stuart sly-dog,
Friend of fiery Fletcher,
Scots land-owner,
Smuggles him aboard
A frigate, persuades weavers,
Makers and menders of shoes,
The soldiers he's stuck with,
He's bound for Bristol,
'A trial when we take Bristol'.

Lies from the royal lips,
Lies to men die for him,
Fletcher's bound for Bilbao.

And worse, sly mouth entices
Local pilot, John Kerridge,
To guide the frigate to the deep
And to the 'trial' in Bristol.

Poor Kerridge, carried
To Bilbao, arrested, gaoled
A year, shipped back,
Tried as traitor, is lucky
To win pardon. Home,
He stays ashore.

Fletcher did better –
Ended up a Scottish MP,
A man who helped shaft
A republic for a horse.

Motif

It's getting to be a motif.
You walk the heavy-pebbled beach
At Lyme and say, round here,
The scaffolds, Monmouth's men
Hanged, disembowelled, chopped up.

Then someone shows you a fossil.
A hundred and ninety million years old,
Suddenly extinct. You eat
Fresh plaice from ancient sea.

Darwin, and the foxes crushed
On asphalt, teach life is cruel.
You lean back in yourself,
In a sun-spot where the waitress
Gets less than minimum wage,
Where the tea was picked by pickers
Whose suffering you could look up,
While your body perhaps rebels
Raising disease in hidden interstices.

And all you can say is,
Yes. Drink up. Drive on.

Second Sign : The Raid on Bridport, 14 June 1685

Expecting Christ, his warrior-Lord,
To descend from golden cloud
On a silver, celestial stallion,
Sword, armour, eyes, ashine,
At any minute, Samuel Venner,
Marched his men through mist
To kill militiamen at Bridport.

Lord Grey, wenching-companion
To Monmouth, cavalier fop,
Inexplicable right hand man,
Not expecting to see Christ
Either side of the hated grave,
Scared of gunshot, led the Horse.
Historians wonder why he'd come,
But a king's pal can clean up
On money, land and crumpet.

Venner stormed Bridport Bridge,
Stormed the militia off
The wide, rope-hanging street.
Fired at, he killed two gentry
In The Bull, thanked Christ
For guiding his bullets home,
Got shot in the gut.

Out of the west, the cavalry
Charged, full-bugle, lumbering-
Hooved cart-horses of war, driven
By L-plate drivers. A volley
Convinced Grey battle folly,
(Some blame horse-panic).

Whatever, sparks flew as they
Lumbering-turned and fled,
Leaving the poor bloody infantry
Where it's usually left –
In the shit. And thick of war.

'The flight of Lord Grey
So discouraged the vanguard
That they threw down their arms
And began to run,' wrote Wade,
Leader of the second wave,
But he regrouped, drew them up
On the bridge, where, my book says,
They swapped insults with militia men,
Safely ensconced at their end of town,
Then marched out, orderly,
Carrying Venner.

Meanwhile, back at the ranch,
Grey galloped in, reported
A massacre by the militia,
'A rout, we had to run'.

Monmouth, bold in crisis,
Pale ditherer in-between,
Saddled his rebel posse.
Charging to the rescue,
He met Wade's marching column,
Its brown and buff jackets
Brightened by redcoat converts,
Seized muskets. His glance at Grey
Must have been quizzical:

A victory of sorts, but a sign
Grey and his cavalry

Cannon to left of them,
Cannon to right of them,
Unlikely to be up for thundering
Into the Valley of Death,

An easy prey
For Jimmy's Hired Guns –
The First Horse Guards,
The Royal Horse Guards,
The King's Own Royal Dragoons,

Booted and spurred
And on their way.

The Catch

Samuel Robbins, poor fisherman,
But in no need of an Enterprise scheme,
When three fine ships sailed into Lyme
Rowed out, offering fish for sale.

The glam, the Proddie Duke,
Questioned him re local loyalty,
The disposition of the militia,
Then bought fresh cod and lobster.

Carted inland, the poor sod,
Too poor to bribe and banned
From pardon for literally landing
With the Duke, excuses fishy,

Hanged at Dorchester.

Monmouth Proclaimed King: Taunton, 20 June 1685

Here's Cookeney, John and Cookeney, John,
Father and son, tailor and tailor
Gone with Monmouth from Lyme.

I guess a man who cuts and sews
Appearance and protection
Would be alert to class, how lace
Relates to owning land, coarse cloth
To breaking clods. A man who's dressed
A lady in fine silk and whistled
For her lord to pay; who's winced
At paupers in their freezing tatters,
Who's watched a conventicle burn,
While the Anglican, in his Babylon smock,
Preached obedience to lord, priest, king,
A man marching beside the son
He's willing to risk, muskets
Heavy in their arms, chanting
'Exalt him that is low, and abase
Him that is high', what did he make
Of King Monmouth in his scarlet coat,
The posh birds of Taunton curtseying,
The crown-embroidered banner?

After the Proclamation

My Lord Grey, who fled the fray
At Bridport, then lied about the lads
Who stayed to fight, my Lord Grey,
Bold when the foe bares perfumed tits,
Who slobbered on the cheeks
Of silly Taunton lasses who think

Battle is flags and blushing curtsies,

My Lord Grey bids us shout 'King Monmouth',

Toss hats and cheer the new-mint king.

I gave him my back and spat.

My leather coat my father wore
For Cromwell is stiff and thick
To blunt a sabre stroke, but I'd toss
It to a beggar ere I'd cheer.
What man is good enough to crown it
Over godly men? Monmouth Duke
Was bad enough, a pretty man
Sits a horse well, easy in a crowd,
Out-runs the strongest village lout,
But Scripture? Steering the state
Between the Catholic pirate ships?
The rain that rusts our blades is steadier
Than him. A Stuart cozens us again.

I'd fart in his teeth, strike back to Lyme,
Dodging the rich oafs in the militia,
But that Babylon's monkey prances
Still on his blood-red throne. Who knows
God's will? Upon the testing ground
Of battle, what the one true Lord
Intends will out, and Bridport's hint
In glory or in gore made clear.

Trudging through Somerset

Rain. Day after night after day,
Rain. Trudging through mud,
Scythes rusting, armour rusting,
Boots sodden. Trudging
Through Somerset and trudging
Back again. Watching
Monmouth pale and twitch,
Pull towns out of his hat,
'We march to Wells.
We march to Bath.
We march to Keynsham.'
All in the bloody rain.

Rumours Monmouth set to run.
Five grand on his head,
He's jumpy as a woman.
Venner urged him dash
To Holland, desert us.
Venner must watch his back
Lest he be fragged.

At Keynsham, a Royal band
Galloped into our camp:
Killed fifteen. Scared us
To flee to Bath,
Monmouth's dinner
Cooling on the pub table,
So fast we fled.

At Bath, a youngster sent
To trumpet-demand surrender,
Shot dead before his blast was out.
Much laughter from the walls.

At Shepton Mallet, a woman
Refused me when I begged
For eggs: 'Leading chicks
To bloody slaughter,'
She spat.

The King's gauntlet
Tightens on our gullets.

The Battle at Phillips Norton: 27 June 1685

At last, we fight the foe!
At last, Christ smiles
On us and savage-smites
The Babylon king.

The redcoat Guards, Pharoah-bold,
Thinking us peasant pap, hurry
Into our trap. Firing from hedges,
We butcher them like rabbits.
The lane runs red with blood.

Charging as they break,
I scythe a sergeant down,
Then stab his throat.
His bubbling curses
Wing him straight to Hell.

Us Taunton weavers,
Putting Grenadiers to flight!
Surely, the Lord of Hosts
Fires Monmouth's heart,
Who's been so woe-begone
He'd hardly speak an order,
And yet today shines forth
A David. His flashing sword,
His rapier mind,
Rout the Philistine.

The Duke of Grafton's horse
Is shot from under his arse.

His lands topple next.

The Battle of Sedgemoor

'What man soever makes a noise shall be knocked
On the head by the next man.' For 'knocked' read
'Musket butt', read 'dead'. Thus Monmouth admonishes,
In the dark, a candle-torch hand-lifted that men
Take courage from his fearless face.

How, so tense, so taut, not to speak, or jangle-jar
Metal on metal, mile after mile, in boots worn-out
By worn-out feet, after days tramping in wind and rain?
A relief at last to strike, let God pass judgement,
And who will He choose but godly men,
Marching for freedom and the Lord?

Seeking out Langmoor Stones, close to Chedzoy corn,
Chaos. Godfrey, local guide, can't find the crossing.
The Langmoor Rhine, forbidding black water,
Might as well be ocean. Chaos. Panic.
Horses pile into each other. Whinny. Metal clangs.
Troopers swear, invoke their maker. A shot rings out.

They are a mile from the royal camp,
A mile from the royal trooper who wakes the camp.
A mile Monmouth hurries the Red regiment along,
Still time, he hopes, to strike, to catch the royals abed,
A sleeping target for yokels with strong arms.
A mile he orders Grey's horse to race along,
To take the Upper Plungeon, and crossing, hurtle
Into the royal tents. All in the dark, remember.

Horses stumble and fall. Men stumble and fall.
But the royals, cider-heads throbbing,
Fall into rows, half-dressed but musket ready.

Shit-scared, but disciplined. Compton's Blues
Drive Grey away from the Plungeon. In panic,
He races his troopers across the Royal front,
Who fire, terrifying the untrained mares, carthorses,
Peace-loving beasts on which his men are mounted.
Barging out of the dark, the crashing volleys,
Grey's cavalry charge into their own men,
Breaking lines, breaking arms and legs,
Breaking whatever is left of Monmouth's heart.

Chaos. With worse to come. 'Flee, flee
For your lives,' the fleeing cavalry
Shout to the ammo train parked by a farm,
Who promptly do. Wouldn't you,
If a white-faced man on a thundering horse
Yelled as the dark spat him into and out of
Your trembling view?

It begins to look as if God is a Papist,
Or has the hots for tyrant kings. Some slip away
In the melee, but most march on till eerie glow
Disturbs, lengthening in mist. The matches
Of Dumbarton's musketeers smouldering,
Poised to fizzle in the pan. It makes a target
For the rebel van. The Red regiment halt

Facing the foggy light, refuse to budge.
The Yellow bang into them, refuse to budge,
And worse, bang off volley after volley
At the mystery glow.
Firing, they fire high, do hardly any damage.
Amateur soldiers, unused to musket
Crashing back, firing high over the dark-hid foe.

Not that the royals are laughing.
'Fucking peasants.'
For Monmouth's Dutch gunner plies three small cannon,
Sends heads and limbs flying like crippled birds
Among Dumbarton's men, who nearly break.
Nearly. But the royals horse up six huge guns,
Quickly pounding the rebel cannon to bits,
Then open up, with canister, on the rebs.

Imagine standing there, powder running out,
With a savage thirst and loosening bowels,
As balls rip through the ranks and royal muskets,
Aiming low, wreak havoc. The stink of blood, of powder,
The howls of pain, sudden illuminating flashes
Of here an eye, there a leg, blown away.
You can't. But they do, with Monmouth at their head,
Half-pike in hand.

As dawn begins to break, lighting up the many dead,
And ammo near runs out, the Duke remarks to Grey,
Who's stayed to fight, though his troopers fled the field,
'All the world cannot stop those fellows, they'll run presently'.

And so they gallop off, a cheering sight, no doubt,
To men from weaving sheds, on foot, and face it, fucked.

For ninety minutes or more the rebels endure,
Firing high, shouting psalms and imprecations.
Unimaginably brave.

But when the Royal cavalry charge their flanks
The pikes 'begin to shake, and at last open,' the sign
Of breaking ranks, of men running for home, for wife
And child, while the red-coat royal troops,

Till now on hold, swarm across the Bussex Rhine,
Chop them down on the moor, in the Chedzoy corn,
Hang them high in St. Mary's church, chain them
To await Judge Jeffrey's gibbet.

Brave men in the dark, firing high.
A carthorse cavalry.

They did their best.

It wasn't good enough.

And England stuck with monarch, church and class.

Warning Shot, Sedgemoor: 6 July 1685

If it hadn't gone off, that shot,
Historians dispute who triggered it,
Treacherous rebel, or nervous cavalier,
Who knows, Monmouth's men
Might have fallen on the royals,
Bashed skulls, slaughtered troops
Righteously in bloody beds
And Sedgemoor reshaped history.

A more equal society,
No kids hung above looms
In Victorian slavery sheds;
'The Peterloo massacre'
An uncoined phrase;
Empire spurned
And the trench slaughter
Of its young, their descended features
'Just like his dad,' buried in the mud,
Their descendants buried in their balls,
Would not have recruited a single poem.

Or else, that Puritan urge
Might have closed all the pubs,
Sent Wordsworth, Shelley, Keats,
To the scaffold for dreams
Of hugging Nature, that scaley serpent,
And banned the flicks'
Incitement to the flesh.

History's only history
When you're looking back:
No iron rule predicts

That gunshot, or the trooper
Shouting twenty times at least,
'Beat your drums the enemy is come.
For the Lord's sake, beat your drums'.
Or Monmouth deciding to run for it.

Not one highly-educated,
Massively-paid, money-trooper
In our merchant banks,
Our think-tanks, galloped
Into the papers shouting
'Flog your shares. The Japs are sunk.
For profit's sake, flog your shares'.

And though it's not like your brain
Being bashed in with a musket butt,
As you cower in the corn near Chedzoy,
My Somerset mate faces old age's bayonet
Defenceless, his pension blown,
Invested in Japanese industry,
The rising graph that fell on its face
In the whispering silicon,
As the markets aimed their gun.

We march in the dark,
Following the next man:
Our hopes are high
And then the shot rings out,
And then the shot rings out.

A Monmouth Dog

Adam Wheeler, Wiltshire Militia,
Reported a rebel prisoner to be
'Very remarkable and to be admired,
For being shot through the shoulder
And wounded in the belly, he lay
On his Back in the sun stript naked,
For the space of ten or eleven hours
In that scorching hot day, to the admiration
Of all the Spectators; and as he lay,
A great Crowd of Soldiers came about him
And reproached him, calling him
Thou Monmouth Dog'.

Later, they took pity. Impressed
By his bravery, they 'gave him a pair
Of drawers to cover his nakedness'.

He died that night.

Holy Test

'The holy test of pike and gun'
Failed. My Lord why hast?
The huge hole in my side
Is Hellmouth proves Hell
No lie, but here and now
In Chedzoy corn. To never
Hear Margaret sing again,
Nor see my boy, timid,
Mastering his hens,
To die like a rat
At harvest, flung aside
In a field. A Papist king
Pisses on my heart.

Reprisal

They lynch the Dutch gunner,
Then one hundred men:
In His Majesty's words,
'For a terror to the rest'.

At Guantanamo Bay,
The hostages endure
Another year of kidnap:
'For a terror to the rest'.

Bloody

The cliché cavalry charge
Is a bold, brave gallop,
Tennyson-style, lance piercing,
Sword slashing, poor bloody infantry
Bloodied and breaking.

But here, 'advance at a trot,
A brisk steady pace,'
Plenty of time to wonder why
You hadn't joined the foot,
Their hedgehog pikes bristling,
Muskets blasting at you
Long before your pistol
Pops. Plenty of time
To wish you'd been born
After the tank was invented,
All that armour around you
And a bloody great gun.

Failing to foresee bazooka,
Wire-guided missile,
Flesh melting in furnace-heat,
Boiled in your own water.

Failing to forget the past,
Its live testosterone rush:
Shoulder to brotherly shoulder
A troop of shag-pelted men
Charge down a Neanderthal.

A King in a Ditch: Horton Heath, 8 July 1685

A king in a ditch,
A ditch round a king.
Thorn protects:
Thorn hurts.
Nettles hide:
Nettles hurt.
That the gentry stayed home,
Delamere, Strode,
Locked in their fine houses,
Loath to risk losing, hurts.
That he should have stayed home,
Locked in Henrietta's bosom,
Pink-nippled, but hunger,
Hunger unsated by a pocket
Of stolen peas, grass chewed,
Muddy puddle water
No claret substitute,
Dressed in rags,
Shaking, all atremble
Like a first-fuck girl,
Why, why did We,
Black jest, I,
Leave Holland,
Its damp freedom,
Leave Henrietta,
Her loving bosom,
My hand on her thigh,
God's hand shown
For the Papists,
God a traitor,
Should have stayed home,
Let the land fester,

The Maids of Taunton
Bending their knees,
The cheers at Lyme,
I stink, I tremble,
Put slug to lips
But can't eat,
Grey a coward,
Brave men breaking
Under Feversham's guns,
A head on the moor
I tripped on, blood
On my boots, its one eye
Staring, her loving bosom,
That Cheapside wench
That Grey and I
Took turns to ride,
Her moans, my moans
I stifle with bracken,
Her bucking hips,
Never again, never again
The women, the cheers,
The fine gesture,
'Why Sir, if you'll not tip
To me, then I must
Tip my hat to you,'
Doffing my plume
To three Quakers,
The crowd cheer,
Girls' eyes glisten,
My tyrant uncle,
His Papist majesty,
The axe, the sharp axe.

In his Pomp

'In his pomp,' Venables said,
Of the shot shot wide,
'Matteus would have put that away,
Made Man United suffer.'

In his pomp, Monmouth
Had the West Country at his feet,
Made Somerset united,
Made Somerset suffer.

At the last, he knelt
To Jack Ketch, butcher,
By royal appointment.

Eight blows to sever his head.

Reading History

Here, on the beach, west of the Cobb,
They landed, Monmouth and 82 men,
Eager to free England. Not sure how.
A bit like Clinton in Kosovo.
Hoping for a rising;
Hoping for a gentry cavalry
Riding out of the West;
Hoping old Jamie Milosevice
Would do the decent, hand over
His land to the Proddy dog.
Hoping.

'Stupid,' Earle brands Monmouth:
'Dickhead,' some see Clinton.
But to Clifton, Monmouth's a man
Matured from Blade-doggery,
Honour-trapped, even devout,
At ease with folk not court-bought,
Tipping his hat to a Quaker
Who had refused to tip his to him,
A gesture thrills a crowd,
Hints freedom to worship as you will
Free of bishops and gentry if you will,
Which hints, to some, equality,
Levelling, which kept the gentry
Sitting on their hands, not saddling up
Till it was clear the King would win,
And then they rode for James,
Sent in their fighters. Not that NATO
Even hints equality, so the rich
Are all for putting the boot in.

A purple-clad prince, affable
In a Dorset port going broke,
A place where little happens,
Was bound to draw a crowd.
Fishermen, weavers, unemployed,
Flocked in, shouldered guns, scythes,
Rode the thrill of a righteous crowd,
How lose with the Lamb on your side?

But God, like history, backs the victor.
Forget the ifs and buts, academic replays
Of the ends-in-tears campaign,
The King's cavalry swung Sedgemoor,
Frightening as an F16
To tired men on foot, whose hopes
And blood ran out among the corn.

Here on the beach, west of the Cobb,
Where crowds from Brum
Decide to go to Spain next year,
'That Cobb's not up to much,
Not like in the film,
And besides, you get the sun,'
The scaffold stood, the young men
Hanged till not quite dead,
'Their Privy Members cut off,'
Disembowelled, beheaded,
Trunks quartered, boiled, pickled,
In front of friends and gentry,
To teach them a lesson.

A cluster bomb is quicker:
Effects worse.

Parry says horses refused to tow the sled
The soon to be dead were mounted on.
The crowd took it as a sign
God still, discreetly, on their side.

Some Kosovans think NATO flies for Allah.

How did they explain the King's army,
Kirke's 'Lambs', let loose on the West
Like Serbs in Kosovo,
Raping, looting, killing,
For the sheer bloody fun of it
And to maintain the King's peace?

Work of the devil, I guess.

And the eight strikes of the axe
Failing to sever Monmouth's head?

A sign he wasn't meant to die.

And the bombed TV station?

A sign that NATO means to win.

Alice Lisle

Back of the church, we skulk,
A posh wedding out front,
Waiting the bride, white Roller,
While we're looking for Alice Lisle,
Her tomb. How search graves
When bride flaunts fertility
In blossom-white, bright May?

Weeds clarify eyes. Blade-leaves
Resist tread. Birds shout from yew
So big. The country still exists,
Unfarmed, in church back yards.

At last, snaps taken, they're in,
Hectored by the vicar to sing,
To celebrate this union
Evens to end in divorce.

We find the brick box holds
Whatever's left of Alice Lisle,
Seventy year old, posh Lady,
The King wanted to burn,
But in his mercy, sceptred grace,
Said, 'OK, chop her head off.
Tomorrow, Winchester market.
Teach neighbours an audio-visual
Lesson : don't mess with me.'

Focussing my lens, two buttercups,
Something blue, frail flowers
Some kid I guess has plucked,
And left, called in to watch

The splicing of the bride,
Leaving their stems to die
Upon these eroding words,

    'Alicia Lisle,
Died 2 September 1685'.

Bloody times. But look,
See the old lady lives alone,
Just down your street, my road,
Unvisited, each day a chopping off
Of mind from trunk of past,
A bride once, a mother still, and ask,
Which days loom worse,
The day of execution
Or the bloodless empty day
After bloodless empty day?

And no indignant historian
To tell your end.

After Sedgemoor

Heads that shouted lustily, 'A Monmouth!'
Limbs that bloodied the Grenadier guards,
Ended up parboiled in bay-salt, cummin seed,
(The odd particularity of research)
'To keep them from putrefaction ...
To keep off the fowles from seizing on them'.

So thoughtful, nailed on poles
In the not-yet-pretty villages,
Where now cream teas are served
To tourists keen on heritage.
The daily sight and stench,
(You really think those herbs had much effect?)
Reminding the guys and gals
'Wherever you go, we know your address'.

Imagine getting the milk in,
Taking the mail off the postman,
While a large chunk of what was your son
Wafts in the breeze.

Wiveliscombe

One reading of Wiveliscombe
Is 'weevil-infested valley',
But it wasn't weevils infested
The ciderous combes of Somerset,
Just pickled heads and chunks
Of bodies, hanging from gates,
Trees, pub-signs, churches.

Collateral Damage

Of the victorious soldiery, Earle writes:
'They raped, pillaged, and bullied'.

And my affable mate, pipe in mouth,
Told me how, conscripted to Malaya,
He was made to take part in a platoon
Gang bang. Fourteen men taking their turn
To rape a girl whose dad's a Communist.

In Vietnam, a new fellatio:
'The girl sucked a rifle-barrel
And had her brains blown out'.

'Things in khaki,' Lawrence wrote.

Men.

Imagine

Imagine you're from Wilton, Wilts:
Never been further than Salisbury:

Imagine you and the constable at odds over a girl:
Imagine he reports you absent at Monmouth's rebellion,

Knowing you to have been drunk in Salisbury:
Imagine soldiers knock you about a bit:

Imagine you're taken to Taunton, a town
You've never visited, to face Hanging-Judge Jeffreys:

Imagine his abuse; imagine being taken
Through the red-earth paradise of Taunton Dene,

The fruitfullest fruitfields of England,
Roped, in a cart, through villages where sullen

Villagers are made to shout 'God save King James,'
By redcoat savages knock them about a bit.

Imagine knowing it's the last day you'll see green.
Imagine climbing out at Stogumber, a little place,

And climbing the scaffold saying your prayers.
Imagine that. For something similar,

In the essentials and the gasping end
Happened to Lockston, John, of Wilton, 'absent',

Tried at Taunton, hanged at Stogumber.
Even if he had no girl and fired a gun.

Shock and Awe

For nine months, the West
Was Falluja. Just being there
Made you a target. Soldiers beat
Whoever could not pay them not to:
With little luxury to plunder,
They settled for rape. 'Made one
Entire bawdy house of ye West
Of England.'

Nine months of retribution.
And, after nine months, to bear
Your rapist's child.

'That'll learn yer.'

A lesson much taught in Serbia
And Afghanistan.

The Bureaucracy of Pain I

After the Battle of Sedgemoor,
To kill four rebels at Bath required:
Rope to throttle them;
Firewood to burn their bowels;
A furnace to boil their heads
And hacked off quarters;
Two pecks of salt for pickling,
And spears and poles on which to stick
The boiled and pickled product.

'A macabre postscript shows
That the writer nearly forgot an axe
And a cleaver would be required,'
Just one of each, to use four times.

Four oxen and a cart:
A guard of forty troopers.

And oh! We mustn't forget:
Four men.

The Bureaucracy of Pain II

In town after town,
That highest faculty of man,
Sweet reason in its matrix-making,
List-processing power, sat down
To plan and cost the implements,
Right down to the posts
On which to stick severed heads,
And decide, with careful thought
For maximum, cost-effective visibility,
The best spots at which to hang
The hacked-off chunks of men.

In Weymouth:

'At the grand Piere:
Six quarters and a head'.

Try snogging under that!

'At the towne's end:
Two quarters',

To bid farewell and welcome.

'Neere the Windmill:
Four quarters and one head',
That candy-floss
Remain unsold
To the good
Of ye nation's teeth.

The Bureaucracy of Pain III

Not cheap, state terrorism.
At Weymouth, Clifford calculates,
Execution cost 27 shillings a man.

This at a time when yearly income
For a labouring man was 4 pound ten shillings.

Or, to put it another way,
Roughly four months of labouring
In wind, sun and rain,
Of sometimes singing,
Buy the thirty minutes or so
To butcher a man.

The Bureaucracy of Pain IV

12 at Weymouth
At 27 shillings a head
Is 16 pounds and 4 shillings.

More than a farmer,
A shopkeeper, a clergyman
Or an army officer
Made in a year.

Not Taken

'Out in the rebellion and not taken.'
Drake, Daniel, of Buckland St. Mary,
Drake, George, of Buckland St. Mary,
Drake, Henry, of Buckland St. Mary.

Escaped?

Or thrown into the bloody pit
Dug to bury bodies stripped
Of plunder.

From Daniel, imagine a buff coat,
A stale crust in the pocket,
Grabbed by a grenadier.

From George, a broadsheet ballad,
'England's Darling', praising Monmouth –

>   'Young Jemmy is a youth
>   who thinks it no transgression
>   To stand up for the Truth
>   and Protestant Profession:
>   And oh! he fights with such success
>   all mortal powers obey,
>   No god of war but must confess
>   Young Jemmy bears the sway.'

Sneer-sung by a trooper to his mates
Then force-swapped for another round of cider
From a frightened tavern-keeper
Who chucks it on the fire.

While Henry lies grinning,
The kerchief given by a girl
Too bloody to be taken,
Red around his sabred head.

What's in a Name?

Six or seven, can't be sure, John Parsons
Fought the parson. Two were hanged.
Two shipped to Jamaica. One,
Sentenced to be shipped, never,
Can't be sure, got on the boat.
One, can't be sure, sabred or shot,
Killed at Sedgemoor.

Best Friend

One of the few big knobs
To come out for Monmouth,
William Plumley, lord
Of the manor of Locking,
Fought at and escaped from

Sedgemoor. Got home.
Hid. But when Kirke's Lambs
Broke in, his dog betrayed
His hiding place.

Rebellion, perhaps, is catching:
The book blames 'excess devotion'.

Plumley hanged.

Aftermath

Just think of the back-handers, the beddings,
When parish officials, King's Men all,
Conjured up lists of those 'levying
War against the King', 'being out
In the horrid rebellion', 'absent from
His home', 'being a terrorist',
'Being a Muslim'. The outcome:

A fixed trial and execution,
Or rendering to the Caribee.

Small Mercy

Tripp, Jacob, twenty-one,
Tried at Wells, sentenced
To hang at Axbridge,
But, 'being unconscious
And dying of gaol fever'
Was hanged in the market
At Wells.

Waste not, want not.

Pour Encourager les Autres

Luscombe, William, of Wallington,
'In prison for rebellion', maybe taken
Armed and heading for Monmouth,
Was hanged as Ruscombe
At Wiveliscombe, a place still
Just a few dots on the map,
A place without even one
Certified rebel, but the villagers
Were drummed and clobbered out
To watch him be butchered
And saw and smelt him nearly a year.

They got his name wrong:
They may have got his guilt wrong:
But he was poor and a Somerset man
Who would do to frighten a yokel or two.

Christopher Battiscombe

Amidst state terror, the red-faced judge
Drenching the West in Stuart napalm,
Many died in good cheer. 'Farewell,
Temporal inheritance, I am going
To my heavenly eternal one,' cried
Christopher Battiscombe, Dorset lawyer,
Fighter for Christ, from the cart
Carrying him to the scaffold.

I'd like to confirm MacNeice,
'It was all so unimaginably different,
And all so long ago', but, checking
The index, learn his brother, Peter,
Solid rock, sought the grant of his estate,
'Having always been faithful', rejecting
The 'traiterous practices of his brother'.

Stuka

Hanging Judge Jeffreys
Stukaed the West Country:
Anger his siren,
Axe and rope his bomb.

Should've been shot down.

On Yer Cart

Hucker, John, sergemaker,
Captain of Horse, they hanged
In front of his home crowd
At Taunton. Let them see
Their mighty dissident
Dangle.

Hurford, Cornelius,
Humble man, trade
Unknown, of Wellington,
They hanged high
In South Petherton.
Why?

In the list of rebels
By residence
South Petherton looms large,
Though small on the map.
Three transported; three hanged,
And twenty-one 'in the rebellion
And not come in', twenty-one
Either dead or on the run.

Clearly, South Petherton
Needed a slap. And clearly,
Its men didn't proffer
Their cheeks. But why
Hang the South Petherton
Three, two at Wincanton,
One at Pensford?

Pensford is tiny.

No rebels are known.

There must have been a plan,
Though no book mentions it,
To hang a man wherever
Two or three were gathered,
A sort of terrorist tig,
The hamlets being it.

Imagine the long hours
Some poor sod spent
Matching necks to slots,
No computer to assist,
The to-and-fro of carts,
The cock-ups, as the wrong man
Was Parcel-Forced
To the wrong address
And strung up anyway.

Hanged men,
And bits of hanged men,
Ubiquitous
As cream tea signs
And cider come-ons
On the tourist route.

Sniff me and stop home.

The Lesson

A Sedgemoor rebel, quartered,
Could hang out at four addresses,
Terrorise four villages on the cheap.

'But that was centuries ago.
Good God man, have a drink.'

During the Mau-Mau revolt,
The hanged bodies of black men
Were cut in two, hung up one
Each side of town, or displayed
At crossroads to deter.

The continuities of history:
Economy and brutality.

Bad Folks

Jeffreys hanged them:
Divvied out their cash.
Bush bombed them:
Divvied out their oil.

Tatterdemalion

'Tatterdemalion', one historian's sneer
At Dorset rebels in their ragged gear.
Its five syllables reek of Common Room
Hatred of common man, as if the loom
Weavers, shoe-makers, fullers, who fought
Deserve no credit for searching thought
About Bible, God and man. The genteel sniff
That, bumpkins, they were spun into a tiff,
Or fell for Monmouth in his purple coat.
It's that supercilious, sneering note
Tells us why rebels wanted to shut down
Oxbridge, to tear off priests' and lawyers' gown,
To build a republic. It wasn't fashion:
A hate of hierarchy fired their passion.
It still exists. In just-acquired, spire-
Boasting T-shirt, beginning to enquire
The cost of paper, pen and Oxford guide,
My Zambian friend was shocked and mortified
When the girl on the till pointed and spat;
'You're new here aren't you? Won't be wearing that
When you realise how much we locals hate
The university. I'd burn it, mate.'

Revenge

In a literal savage twist,
Cornish, London alderman,
Suspect conspirator, was hanged,
At King James' command,
'In sight of his house', a rich one,
'His head placed over Guildhall'.

Imagine the royal chuckle,
'Let him look his last on what he's lost.

And those damn Whig merchants,
Let 'em watch his plotting head rot down.'

Weaving History

Three weavers from Stoke Trister, tiny hamlet,
All called Bollster, Edward, Israel and James,
Fought at Sedgemoor, the last battle on English soil
My history book says,

Sick of weaving, perhaps, to keep a clothier rich:
Devout men, fearing a Papist king force-feeding them
Wine and wafer: village men, eager for pike-thrust:
The chance to cut a lace-wrapped throat,
To lift a silk gown,

Maybe all six, in different mixes,
In each rebellious man,

Stumbled through the dark, to pre-dawn battle,
Raised pike and psalm against gun blast and cavalry.

Edward and James, the book says, were billed
'At large or killed' at the assize. Let's hope
At least one ran to the wild wood, changed name
And game, joined a band of unruly men
Who 'Refuseth the king's law'.

Israel of Stoke Trister, guilty of rebellion,
Was given to Howard, face-in-the-trough
Jamaica Governor, as a perk.
Imagine his trip from misty Somerset,
Clacking loom, to sun-struck servitude,
Boiling sugar, bossing blacks about.

Not knowing their end, I glance at the paper:
The boss of Barclays leaves with four million,

His perk for sacking ten thousand.

On a Weymouth estate, Tim Weaver, small boy,
Sharpens his hatred, scratches the Merc
Of the guy who lifts his single mother's skirt
For twenty quid.

The battle goes on.

Their Names Liveth After

Burton, James, of London,
From Holland with Monmouth,
Lieutenant of Horse,
True Prot or fortuneseeker
The book doesn't say,
And life could cast him both,
Banged up in Newgate,
'Interrogated', a word
Conjures heat and pain,
Chains and pincers,
The book doesn't say,
Turned King's Evidence,
Royal stoolie, ratted on
Two who gave him shelter,
Elizabeth Gaunt,
Burnt at the stake,
John Fernley,
Hanged by the neck.

More than their names,
Their savage fate,
The book doesn't say,
And I wonder
As torch bent to kindling,
What Elizabeth thought
Of the man she gave eggs,
And maybe shared
Whatever hay, board or truckle
Passed for her bed with,
Before all thought was burnt out,
And whether, as the rope
Chafed his neck,

John Fernley prayed
Forgiveness for the man
He helped, the man
Rewarded with liberty,
Let loose in London to ...

The book doesn't say.

Political Terrorism

Of Elizabeth Gaunt,
Parry reveals:

'This poor woman's story is perhaps even more pitiable than
that of Alice Lisle. Elizabeth was the wife of William
Gaunt, a yeoman of St. Mary's, Whitechapel ... she was an
Anabaptist, a sect much detested by Anglicans, Tories and
Royalists. She was well known at Wapping, and in the east
of London, as a woman of godly and charitable disposition.
She spent much of her time in visiting the poor of all per-
suasions, and often entered Newgate and other prisons to
minister to those in distress.'

In this sex-mad age,
You can't really imagine
A Christ-mad one,
Not that Christ
Was in the judge's heart,
The chance to kill
Whig Sheriff, Cornish,
Ring, a rebel,
Fernley, a barber,
And Gaunt,
Religious nutter,
Leveller, heaven-sent.

'A master stroke of political terrorism to bring the Whigs
and Dissenters ... to a wholesome fear of the law' is Parry's
comment.

Our glorious heritage.

Burton was found up
Fernley's chimney,
From which he fell,
Soot-suited.

And here's a laugh,
Two of Fernley's witnesses,
Mr. Haddock and Mr. Dove,
Refused to testify
To help their friend,
Feared the court's wrath
Would savage them.

Gaunt, it seems,
On Mrs. Burton's word,
In a rigged trial,
Had given not eggs
But five pounds charity
To Burton. Proof?
How can there be?
But clearly treason.

The night before she burnt
Elizabeth wrote:

'I did but relieve a poor unworthy and distressed family, and
lo, I must die for it. I desire in the Lamb-like will, to forgive
all that are concerned and to say, Lord, lay it not to their
charge. But I fear and believe that when he comes to make
inquisition for blood, mine will be found at the door of the
furious judge, who, because I could not remember things
through my dauntedness at Burton's wife's and daughter's
witness, and my ignorance,took advantage thereat and
would not hear me, when I had called to mind that which I
am sure would have invalidated their evidence; and though
he granted some things of the same nature to another, yet he
granted it not to me.'

At the burning:

'The victim was not strangled, as was sometimes done out
of mercy, but she was literally burned alive as the judge had
ordered and the King had desired.'

The petty James,
His faith too weak
To trust a trip to hell
For those who rebel,
Bestows a Satanic kiss,
While, later,
He'll snog all Dorset silly
And slip Somerset
A meat injection.

A witness noted:

'That she met her horrible death with calmness and dignity,
arranging the straw about her feet that the flames might do
their work more quickly.'

Christ, as usual,
Did not intervene
Though belief in him
Helped to sustain her.

It is not recorded
If dignity extended
To her bowels.

I fear and believe
The judge paid no price,
Other than being him,
So let's name him,
Wythens,

Jeffrey's hack,
James's toady,
Gaunt's killer,
King's man.

At the Stake

Just think how much it hurts
When steam from the boiling kettle
Catches your pouring hand.

And then think, quite soberly,
Of Elizabeth Gaunt ablaze.

Courage

Here's Speke, who did not,
Of Whitelackington, gent,
Marched with Monmouth,

Offered a pardon

To blab on Prideaux,
Suspect ringleader.

Refused to swear,

Refused to bribe,
Rode down the fear,
Hanged at Ilminster.

And Prideaux,
Of Forde Abbey, rich,
He kept his neck,
And dick, and guts,
Ransomed by his missis
Giving fifteen grand
To grasping Judge Jeffreys.

Does this make Speke a fool?
No more than the Dutch policeman
Refused to round up Jews,

Knowing he would be shot.

And was.

Survivor

Oh handsome he rode with sword and Book,
He promised that God's love would shield him.
A loving man, my side he forsook:
His eyes, his whispers, are decades dim.

He swore that Monmouth's fight would free,
End lords and poverty. Gents grabbed
Our rebel house, they vagabonded me.
To pay my way, I've tricked and drabbed,

Now winter face earns no reward.
In Sedgemoor grave at peace he rests,
Who loved me, but who me bewhored.
Oh Christ, to feel him touch my breast!

Young men are young fools, easily led,
For words and glory they ride greedy.
Now I have a hedgerow for a bed:
The lord of the manor rests easy.

A Visit to Norton St Philip

Stone cottages, so old I thought at first
That Monmouth's men fought down their lane,
But a chisselled date disillusioned me ;
I guessed again as hedges, big and thick
Enough to hide hundreds, who fired on
The redcoat cavalry, killing fifty.

Somewhere on this now affluent street
Holmes, who'd fought for Cromwell,
Suffered his arm shattered by a ball.
Chopped it off himself, with a cleaver
In the kitchen of the tourist-seeking George.
Nine days later he fought at Sedgemoor.

Writing this, checking a map of the battle,
I realise my second-guessing wrong, hedges
Divided fields. Back then, the cottages
Still stood as cottages, though cob and thatch.
Holmes was hanged in September,
And his son died fighting in these fields.

Devotees

Monmouth.
James the Second.
George W. Bush.
Tony Blair.
Osama bin Laden.

Devout men all:
Let us pray,
And count the dead.

Memorial

The land stretches wide and flat and lush.
Beneath a sky shifts from grey to pearl to grey,
Corn grows unbloodied in the humid hush,
Though Chedzoy corn sopped red that day.

The flatness runs for miles until the low flanks
Of the Polden Hills, and, three hundred years back,
Men raced for miles across that flat, ranks
Broken, fleeing from their failed attack.

Only a plaque reminds, not far beneath your feet
Is the mass-grave of hundreds who didn't reach those hills.
You stare down at black canvas, cool in heat,
Of shoes Marks stack in ranks, a sight fulfills

The claim we're all joined-up as middle class.
Imagine those cobblers, weavers, working men
Swapping tools for guns, enlisting en-masse
To fight a king would boss a papist den.

That the rough moor where rebels fought and died
Is parcelled into field and farm is progress,
Few dispute. That your shoes, so brightly tied,
Were glued by kids in Asia working for less,

Is not. Nor is the truth our rich-right speakers
Hide, a third of kids in this green land
Cannot afford to buy your so-cheap sneakers,
Stuck in poverty, the mind's quicksand

Sucks down all hope, all joy, all liberty:
The God fled, who might have helped them fight.
Bombarded by the media flibberty-
Gibberty, the huge images that incite

Longing and self-hate, they take their pills
And blame themselves for being no-one.
Three centuries gone, no racing for the hills.
The land's been parcelled out. They've got none.